MORTAL

mortal

Ivy Alvarez

Red Morning Press

Red Morning Press is an independent publisher of contemporary poetry.
Its partners would like to thank Roxanne Rash and McNaughton & Gunn
Inc., Saline, Mich.

Cover Painting: 'Gimme' (mixed media on canvas), Christine Hamm
(New York, 1999)

Library of Congress Cataloging-in-Publication Data
Library of Congress Control Number: 2006935025
Alvarez, Ivy
Mortal/By Ivy Alvarez
p.cm
ISBN 9780976443926
I. Title

II. Poetry. Creative writing. Myths. Mother-daughter relationship. Illness.
Multicultural studies. Emigration. Immigration.

Red Morning Press
1140 Connecticut Ave., Suite 700, Washington, DC 20036
www.redmorningpress.com
www.myspace.com/redmorningpress

For Ma, Lola Impiang & Lola Rosa

Acknowledgements

Thanks to the editors of *Anon, Babaylan Speaks, Blue Giraffe, bovine free wyoming!, Centoria, Cordite Poetry Review, c-side, Dakota House Journal, Divan, Famous Reporter, 40° South, Lichen, Magma, The Makata, Meanjin, MiPOesias, New England Review, Other Poetry, Perfect Diary 2003, Poetrix, Poetry Wales, Republic Readings, Retort Magazine, Spume, The Stinging Fly, Stylus Poetry Journal, Togatus* and *The Write Stuff*.

Some poems were first broadcast on 5UV, 7ZR, Anna Livia Radio, PoeticA, Radio National, SBS Radio and TTT; podcast on miPOradio and My Vocabulary; compiled for the *TOG* audio CD (2000); included in SBS's *Whatever* (Artiste in Residence) online program; and published in the anthology *Moorilla Mosaic: Contemporary Tasmanian Writing* (Hobart: Bumble Bee Books, 2001), in the 1997 Tasmanian Poetry and Dance Festival program, and in two chapbooks, *Food for Humans* (Melbourne: Slow Joe Crow Press, 2002) and *catalogue: life as tableware* (Wales: The Private Press, 2004).

'touch' and 'visit' received a commendation in the 2001 Daffodil Day Arts Awards for Poetry. 'earth' was included in the 2004 Australian/Pacific Region Literacy Placement Test for Scholarships (University of New South Wales).

This book was assisted by a grant from Arts Tasmania through the Premier, Minister for State Development, a residency at the Varuna Writers Centre in the Blue Mountains (Eleanor Dark Foundation) and a grant from The Arvon Foundation for a residency at Moniack Mhor, Scotland.

Thanks to MML Bliss, Angela Rockel, Deb Westbury, WN Herbert, Linda France, Nick Carbó and Denise Duhamel for encouragement and advice, and to Chris Perkowski, Dennis Campbell and Andrew Brown for their support. Special thanks to Mark Heseltine.

Tasmania

Contents

born

they had to unzip me
to let the cat
out the bag

blood bathed my belly
thighs
and baby Seph

I stopped counting stitches
forgave the marring
of my clean envelope

when her suckling cry
murmured at my neck

when the blood in my body
turned to milk

and her gums
took my flesh
her first teeth
nipping like a cat

A sky blue with hysteria, roses blowsy and promiscuous, bees fat-bottomed and buzzing—it is a shaking, baking summer. Dee and Seph eat by the reservoir. The firepit coals sing to the meats roasting above them, which hiss and spit in return. Mother and daughter take a corncob each; shuck off its clothes and yellow filaments. The corns' niblets darken in the heat. Retrieved, salted, cooling, they lie on plates. Seph nibbles on the neat rows, methodical as a typewriter. Ping! With a fingernail, Dee picks out fibres caught between her teeth. Their shoulders brown as an ant crawls off a spear of grass, falls to earth and climbs another.

Demeter and Persephone

The Abduction of Demeter

This time it is Demeter Hades wants. He drags her through the garden, throws her to the ground. It opens like a mouth. Grains scatter from her hand. Persephone knots fists in her mother's skirt. Her heels churn the earth. The wet earth swallows. Demeter disappears. Persephone falls silent. The garden grows cold. Her mother is gone. There is only mud.

Demeter's down below
—the earth is on her: a pressed flower.
A sour breath has filled the hole,

something has her by the throat.
Above, Persephone, her daughter,
waits. Demeter struggles below,

reaps scratched arms, splinters in her soles.
A close gust of laughter
blows its breath inside that hole.

Why is her right hand so cold?
With dirt in her eyes, knots in her hair,
Demeter crawls down below.

She cries. Why is it so cold?
No tongue moves to speak to her
and still this breath that's in the hole,

still a hunger that's swallowed her whole.
She's in the earth and going nowhere.
Demeter lies, waits down below,
holds her breath in that muddy hole.

Persephone presses her ear to earth.
There is no sound, but for grains shifting
to accommodate her ear. Mute mouth. Tongue
stuck, lips shut, the earth turns, the sun inflames
her neck, reddens a cheek as ladybirds
cling to her hair. Midges hum above her
breath. Sandflies lick salt from the edge of her
tears: such thin liquid notes, as sound travels
an ear, draining clockwise, trickling downwards,
to water infinitely each loam-crumb
on its way. Grass blades under her fingers
buoy her palms, her arms, as Persephone
dreams of her fist pushed in that earthy mouth,
of hauling Demeter out—safe, rescued.

Demeter sleeps and waits in the dank earth
as root tendrils tighten knots in her hair.
Millipedes curl and nestle in her ears;
still her eyes oscillate behind her lids.
Something secret ticks on, unstoppable:
a bulb that waits to bud from cold, flowers
in spring. It is a thin song she waits on,
a hum Persephone might make below
her breath as she gathers the corn to her.
She knows that summer hides in winter's face.
A worm butts its head inside her palm's cup,
dislodges a wheat seed, which germinates,
its thin self rising through layers and months,
so that a stalk cracks the soil, turns green, lives.

Dee and the aratilis tree

it's the tree's season
the blushing fruit waits
(distant cousin to a blueberry)

the tree stands for her
her foot-arches grip the sooty bark
she skins her shins

sweat on her upper lip
clean and scentless

she grasps through the furze
that brushes the back of her hand

snaps off two at a time
the red smell of ripe
seeds on her tongue

pictures for looking

we grow into the largeness of our ears,
the length of our fingers. the skeleton
beneath the skin stretches outward to its
bony promise. we grow into our smiles.

we grow out of our teeth. babies making
way for molars, incisors. chipped teeth are
dentally forgotten, enamelised.
cheeks become less like apples. closer to
how skulls should look. chins insistent as smiles.

we grow into our scars, biding their time
like accidents or illness. we outgrow
the mist resting on our shoulders and grow
towards the sun's light as it whitens
the bones knitting soft beneath our brown skin.

as curve of cheek meets curve of chin, we see
ourselves in her, our mother, the missing
one who felt our feet against her walls as we
pushed forward, to feel the light on our skin.

to a daughter born 1920

lit by candlepower
you walk
serenaded by radio

white moths fly by light
whispers of rain
murmurs of thunder

clouds by your ankles
dust on your heels
freckles on your skin

a thin crown of sweat
wreathes your temples
drips into your eyes

your smile
denies
the pain in your breast

your dress covers your body
as cologne
the smell of rot

the way this picture hides you
behind ink and paper
as your daughter traces your face

as we grew

    i

too much walking or running
wore the soles at our feet.
(how?
no day was long enough)
sandals had holes you could poke
a stick through.
           grime lapped
our heels, leaving tidemarks,
but our sweat
        was as clean as salt.

    ii

moths ushered out the butterflies
the dark was too slow
running to catch the light
the cicadas sang on

    iii

nights were for dreaming
the day before
ebbing towards the moon

bend

a thin girl
living in cloud fissures
scoops the fish from between her legs
and waits for the rains to stop

ripples center her feet
and the trees bend, bend

the fruit falls, bursts open,
the seeds dart into the ground

the rain does not stop
in the five minutes it takes
for the man to rain leather
on her back

licks and snaps

the river is a-flood
risen and unfriendly
she can, if she thinks hard enough,
see her friends watch
a dog drowning, floating down
in a dog-ballet
watch them point

there are no fish between her feet
just ripples
and the rain
bending the trees

Seph growing up

a rock-scraped gash
her shin skin split
her school lunch spilled
the scar not hid
earned her curses and vinegar
her bike went under
the car didn't see her
she was scared by its damage
more than her scratches, bloodflecks
when her mother sent her picture in a letter
it was almost good enough
to be her mother

Seph and the matchbox spiders

these boys keep matchbox spiders
not pets but for fights

you can't hug a spider
you either feed it or it dies

no bigger than the first
joint of a finger

dustball with legs
fangs and eyes

Seph likes the boy whose spider
has a fierce lumpen back, tipped red

she thinks
it'll win

it is female
they are hungrier

two boys, two spiders
arena on a stick

the referee's quick eyes and fingers
balance spiders to stay and fight

all eyes between his fingertips touching the stick
(the dopey ones are coaxed)—he's careful not to get bit

the spiders approach, tails up to thread escape
but hunger is stronger

sometimes one might give chase
one end to another

miniature wrestlers, tugging,
a secret handshake shared

killer and killed in one place
last clasp of jaws, poison and eyes

the unlikeliest of winners sometimes
only one will spin a shroud

only one will eat tonight
one day Seph will own a spider

trained to be a winner
with a hunger to match

a memory of bread

There was to be bread in the house: pandesal. Dee had the recipe, the tools and ingredients. The smell of yeast was kneaded into the air, knuckled into roundness and skin-tightness. Oil made the dough-surface glisten as it swelled, a living thing. A dust of crumbs and then a handful of warm bread, smell and taste bound together—sweetening on the tongue.

mother, daughter

mother, wife to a beekeeper
treads the path to honey

fat and puffy like pollen
golden legs, intent hands

arms for a cradle
baby in the first year

life at the hive
honey-keeper, memory-hoarder

silver scissors
a little curl between her fingers

a weft of yellow-white silk
on fragile curve of bone

her daughter, unbidden, unlooses for her
curls, locks, braids

takes up the sceptre
of the bee-keeper, her hair

fair, darkens by the year
then lightens, silky pollen

the beekeeper's wife, the gatherer
ribbons, labels each year

reaps gold at the nape of a neck

linea nigra

i
this is a one-note love song
unwavering

you are a body braced inside me
listening

ii
a siren sounds
and my flesh opens
you leap out
push against me

so eager to start the race
ready to win and break
that finishing line

iii
black thread plumb line
from my navel to my sex
written on my skin

thumbed smudge
that should've disappeared
six months after you appeared
a month earlier than expected

19

dilated

waking from stunned constriction tight curls
of muscle bind break shoulder plates clawed
ribs a nervy corset for my waist
and hips a clenched fist around my thighs my
breath squeezed out my brain beating fit to
burst

and when my thought is no sturdier
than a blurred bubble the jaw dislo-
cates to fit me in go my feet first
slipping in the oiled juices breaking
down my flesh I am simmering to
feed

it and on this slow passage up to
encompass my being I notice
the fangs dig for purchase inch over
me dig and prick but I don't feel its
venom I notice it having some
trouble

digesting me we wait it out we
are in this together now I send
positive thoughts you can do it and
it does jaws make their penultimate
accommodations and my shoulders
slip

like mulled wine down a cold throat it goes
easy on my neck and my head is
gone a digested thought

to a daughter born 1948

beehive hair glossy black
lips bee-stung in black and white
eyes framed by cat's eyes
your short smart dress
thigh high

stand still

can't you see your daughter
in those thighs
she shares your eyes

blossoms white and awkward
the fake tree shivers at your touch

the lens winks its eye
you tilt your head
and smile

my first baby

I've carried books
heavier than you

your nappied layers
fit my hip

your grey eyes are flecked
with reflected light

how do I hold you,
I wonder, as I'm holding you

when your mother
takes you back

you point your tongue
little arrow

that is how you say goodbye

falling in love

she is a slow balloon
swelling

little hands
print out
the skin belly
palming the walls

(a foot tests the bladder
like a tyre-kicker—
trying it on for size)

she swells and waits
then... deflates

her skin wrinkles soft
impressed by fingers
of the other skin
inside her

the jonquil

the jonquil bulb is growing.
I'm forcing it
in a clear glass vase

little white fringeling fingers
grow down
tipped with yellow
and move a little
below the water's surface

only a matter of time
only a question of when
the fingers will curl in
and under
twist and move around
each other
filling in
the space of the vase

by that time
a single white jonquil
with yellow trumpeting throat
will blow
quite soft and low
a white jonquil scent.

fossil

the day of her arrival is a fossil.
exposed, it erodes
it crumbles apart
grain by grain

this grain is the metal mouth of the aircraft
the attendant is on autopilot and leads her in, blank and smiling

this grain is the plane
scrying over a landscape of night and day

this grain is the tarmac-memory on which she stands
she watches the wind harden in the windsock-mouth

this grain is her mother; 'this is your new home,' she cries out,
her cries and her smiles are mixed in her mouth; fears for her child

ten grains equal ten years
left behind.
the grains fall,
become one with the dust.

fall

Dee's photo in Seph's pocket
mimics her smile. She leaves her
kisses and salt for the three
years away. Seph stands, accepts,
then says, You'll have to learn
to be my mother again. Dee's eyes
wrinkle. Her smile looks fake.

They board the plane. Air pockets
press in Seph's ear. Dee finds her
jellybeans, tells her to chew.

close

chalk dust silt
in the corners of her pockets
little white facts

she paces the thin planks
and her heels echo
at the edge of her skin

moves closer
scratches thought
on a black wall

implacable as seeds
that form
letter by letter

an error of omission
by her hand
swiftly erased

something happened
maybe
an afterthought

the day yawns
slowly
closes its mouth

a memory of worms

Seph loved to scare her mother in the garden by picking up a worm with the tines of her gardening fork and chasing her with it, the dirty-pink body twisting on the end. Dee would scream a little, always eyes on the worm, and run slowly, as if strengthless, a panicked smile on her lips. Seph would laugh. Another day, Dee said she remembered falling in a pit with worms at the bottom. She cried and screamed as they touched her skin. The lavender heads nod in the wind as Dee tells this to Seph.

Seph tells Dee

You don't know anything about flowers,
apart from lavender. These waxy white
ones? Narcissi. Glowing gathered clusters
with small yellow cups. Their scent spills out. Crowned,
each head wears a halo of perfume.
                              Please
don't pick them. Leave their sweet breath to the night—
don't pick them before they're ready to be eased
by gravity, crumpling into the ground.
Soiled root-fingers soon shrink into the bulb,
next season's sugars stored, hoarded like love
never telling until nearly too late.
No—don't pick them, and be picked.
                              Don't tempt fate.

vena cava

when it rains here
I can pretend it's home

outside, the sky is a cloud
and my hand is condensed with water

from touching walls
of earth

roots weave into my hair
I might stay here

learn to love
the rank air

taking my lungs
wipe the slate

clean of rescue

typhoon

rain is always soft here
you'd never feel its spite
know how hard it can drive
stronger than fingers

know that rain can choke you
send you mad
with its constancy
its bitchy everlastingness

touch

I have been told
aches will not be the sign

touch is required
I will feel
the enemy, that rank invader
incubus/parasite
deadly lover

my mother's mother
my mother's sister
knew its touch
my father's father
my father's brother
smelt its breath

breast to breast
it leapt, like lightning
from inner gnawing to outer eye
all along our blood's line

forking like a fault line
across concrete foundations;
every window in the house
cracks wide

where is the sign?

my mother becomes wilfully blind
an ostrich matriarch
who will not feather her finger
along a breast,
scared to find
the mark of the beast

I am suspended in her disbelief

I imagine a long line of dominoes stretch behind us
she will be the last to fall
knock me down with her death's blow

fish hooks

door crack look
my mother's open mouth
the smell of ink

seaweed crush
between my toes
her side wound is a gill

weeping
for lost oxygen
and the time

before it got caught

gen

abbr. 1. gender; 2.a. general, b. generally; 3. genitive; 4. genus; 5. (Bib.) Genesis
n. informal term for information
pref. being born; producing; coming to be
suff. producer; precursor of

she palpates her breast
panic sews her mouth
a grim closed pucker

this, a thin, red thread
through her life, and mine
this pain in the flesh

needles and thread
we live with sharpness
a stitched quilt

hiding multitudes
in our single cells.
we know, don't know

the length of the thread.
some sharp tooth will bite
and snap off the end.

at the doctor's

she asks you to take your clothes off
lie down on the bed
you can paper your nakedness if you wish
the robe is a joke
you both know what you look like

daffodils

for Mark

i

the pinwheel petals have faded
ten suns have shone
and dried the lovely butter colour
a dingy cream

papery crenellated petals, thin
nearly transparent as a Japanese screen

ii

once, they were
green-fleshed crunchy tube-stems
now they are limp
with split, pale, upcurling feet

old yellow heavy heads
overbig, on single stems
droop heavier and heavier still
until chins rest on slender chests

breast

my skin is written
in a limited language
only natives understand

the ink hurts my nerves
I scream
scaring the medicine woman
who needs the tattoos
to guide
and show where to incise
excise

the skin parts like a lipless mouth
speechifying blood

and when all talk is done
my scar is the last punctuation mark.

visit

such soft stems these flowers have
the white bed foils them
the colours luminesce
my mother does not need them

her eyelids are hued by violets
the freckles on her face are the dots
disappearing down an orchid's throat
her mouth is agape, white sap
gathered at the corners

barbed wire scars at her throat
rim the neck of her white
and flowered nightdress
silver-stamened needles
stab her wrists

her left forefinger
pulses
with the life of poppies
killing her pain

water feeds down from a plastic tube

wires enclose her like roots
sucking at the earth

she gives the nurses
nightmares

get-well cards
splay on the wall

dust and petals ring the vases
full of flowers

the barren rose-bush

there's a near-barren rose-bush
straggled in a heap,
clumping untidily
the steps of a garden.

pale exhausted blooms open weary to the sun
pink, overblown

slow-witted insects—midges and bees
butt their heads on the dark buds;

impotent swarm.
some buds have a failing

and will die,
withering on the vine,
never opened.

unwanted

some drug sings in my limbs
a chemical embrace

there's my daughter
crying after me

I'm not myself
bruised fruit

my mouth is lax
I cannot speak

and I repeat myself
and I repeat myself

she fetches pad and pen
I write apologies

her distress is distant
a dropped stone in a well

and I'm at the tunnel's end
waving

43

save

her cousins are in the river
washing the living room rug

blue woolly jewel full of froth
the river slaps its banks

stones settle underwater, underfoot
suds drift like thought

a small procession floats to shore
night flowers, the scent of wood

lost flesh

i

here's the bed she lies in
the sheets might as well be snow
she's so cold
the heat disperses above her
the ceiling blankly accepts it
she sinks clean as a stone

ii

when she wakes there's a scar
where a breast used to be
she shows it to me
excoriated and raw
her eyes shine

iii

when we cross the street
she holds onto my hand
as if I was ten again
and things were still to happen

passage

We're under the bridge.
Why not stay?
Sun's gone from our eyes.

Below the traffic,
we're walking
just above water.

The path's algae-slick.
Better I
drown than you fall in.

The slapping water
tires our dog.
His tongue begs my hand.

We three proceed. Then,
in our eyes,
a sharp cut of sun.

to a daughter born 1974

in your dusky blue dress
you lean
laughing

in its low cut
the curve of a breast

of gods & insects

a drift of wall dust. carcass husks, strung, juice
sucked. small wings beat slow—slower than breath. one
thing picks through the webs. another twitches
nervelessly, invoking death, who comes, swift
electricity to one's nakedness,
gathers the threads, clicks on the loom, shears off
what is not needed

a memory of breasts

I show my mother a book of breasts. At first, she's
shocked and pulls away. But then, she returns to
them and looks at the pictures on the cover. She
points to one. The breasts are creamy and
voluptuous, arms gloved to the elbows, crossed in
front. 'I like these ones,' she says. 'They are elegant.'

wink

season spilling into season
in between winter and spring
spring and summer
something about the blue
that I know, have always known,
pulls away, the closest of winter
skies retreats; a blank face

someone crosses the room
the threshold and out
moving off, as if after a kiss. Goodbye,
and the clouds intercede, the sun pours
over the earth a warm air
that sticks to the walls
long after the rays
wink behind the mountain

risen

Dee's chair receives her
regal and tender the green
brush against skin embroidering its
print flesh insensate
as risen dough I imagine
the yeast-smell of morphine smudges her
eyes to bruise she sits
breast bare like the belly
she once showed me smooth then scarred and waits
for my sponge to clean
her from the blood-crusts of fresh
stitches the pus yellow like yolk her
room acts like she's not
been away my thighs strain from
the weight of my body kneeling I
wet the towel's edge
rough on the skin's frilled edges
wince and suck of breath that hurts she says
stop my arms are
not what they should be my hands
are wet watered blooded her body's
excretions and I mumble
sorry will my hands
take her split mended flesh be gentle

length

I could collect
basketfuls of my hair
knit a little rug
from what I've shed

you could weave a carpet
lay down whole rooms
a house
down the street
and out into the highway
with yours

a full twenty years on me
plus the chemotherapy
you've got a head start

the miles you could've covered
with your hair

matrilineage

her mother shows her a ritual
with her first blood
soap and water

did her mother show this to her
did her mother show this to her and ask
that she show it to her daughter
who will show it to her daughter

that is my blood in the water
that is our blood in the water
that is all our blood

floating there

Seph

After she's packed, Dee gives me two cacti,
books, coffee, a framed degree, her fourth.

Coaxes this last gift, green blades gleaming,
dormant orchids in black pots, all leaf.

Eggshells a cracked mosaic. The whites shine.
'Flowers in spring. They like shade,' Dee said.

Gives me manure, blind to my panic.
Hands make their faltering awkward grab.

'I won't kill these' my hollow mantra.

that second heart

I cannot accept it. How can
one be ready for this gift? My
belly cannot curve to tightness,
my skin cannot hold a drum (that

second heart). I cannot accept
it—limbs bursting buds. I cannot
have the end to blood. I cannot
bear your blood, child, and I think of

you, often.

waiting

the sour-sick smell of another's
breath accumulates
in the yaw of a 747
travelling miles unmeasured
by feet heights unflown
by human arms the lights blink
on the fans blow the warnings
signal blank-faced
attendants at this endless
party while dawn
fingers the elbow resting
on the window
cloud milk condenses
over the country my mother
now sees after gaining wrinkles
grey hair a new air
doors open to tropical
fruits sly pickpocketing
hands the constant press
of smog in her throat
welcoming her like she's
never been away

reunion

we hold
our six breaths
exhale into one

we feel the supple
leather
of our lungs

light
drains the room
into bonelessness

the body bends
into its ritual
shape

aches
to be pliant
and stretched

observes stillness
after a posture
cascade

listen.
the spine talks
the body speaks

a caesura
in each line
a pause for breath

morning

the horns of bread-sellers blow
to greet the dawn
brown boys
who herald the warm pandesal in baskets
on bikes

breadcrumbs crust their fingers
gritty as sand

a sleep-crusted morning
washed down with gritty coffee

the bread yeast smell
rising
like a lazy sun

the bread in my mouth
the sun in my eyes

earth

the rain loves the earth by extinguishing
the sweet burn of day, smoothes the dry furrows
with wet blunt fingers, signals each visit
by taps on the door. it does not forget
to wake the buried seeds warm in their beds,
gently thrums until each pokes out a head
first yellow. darkening when the sun comes

loam crumbs, brown earth melts under water's welts
succumbs to its cool press, the balm of day
gives up the shoots. the stems are gentle spears
beneath the disconnected leaves—
                                          a trail,
a snail gnaws at the tender flesh of stems.
the raindrops follow the curve of its house
glint a sparkle and seep into the ground

resurrection

in the morning, in the winter
ice crusts the earth
frost forms on loamy footpaths,
fishbone leaves,
in the shadow of stones.
the cold needles the flesh of cheeks

then the sun turns up, comes around
a heat presses lightly on the earth
frost beads to water, disperses
lifts in the air, rises
to join the sky
the earth turns, rolls around like a lion caressed
its face directed to the sun
the earth warms
as the temperature rises
by slow degrees

moth

pale white body against the glass
wings pressed towards the light

I am a pulse
I cannot stop beating, beating
so drawn to the alien thing

there is no time to care
the light beckons and I am there

call me ephemeral

soon the crickets will sing their cacophony
and the grass will have my dry wings

light

is the only living thing
breathes life into dust motes
a little god

hooks & nails
draw attention

walls cry out for pictures
sun-fingered curtains
torn wings

a gape of absence

see the dents on the floor
feet once danced here

and tables held books
and chairs held people

ABOUT THE AUTHOR

Born in the Philippines, Ivy Alvarez grew up in Tasmania, Australia. She has held fellowships to both the MacDowell Colony and Hawthornden Castle (UK). She now lives in Cardiff, Wales.